AI PROFIT UNVEILED

A BLUEPRINT FOR EARNING WITH ARTIFICIAL INTELLIGENCE

ALEX USIFO

To my family, whose unwavering support and encouragement have been the bedrock of my journey into the world of artificial intelligence. Your belief in my pursuits has been a constant source of inspiration.

To the dedicated researchers and engineers who tirelessly push the boundaries of AI, thank you for your brilliance and innovation. You are the driving force behind the future we are unraveling.

And to you, the reader, whose curiosity and quest for knowledge have brought you to these pages, may this book spark your imagination and kindle your passion for the limitless possibilities of artificial intelligence.

This book is dedicated to all those who believe in the power of human ingenuity and the transformative potential of AI. Thank you for joining me on this remarkable journey.

CONTENTS

INTRODUCTION

Welcome to the future of wealth creation, where the convergence of data, technology, and human ingenuity is reshaping the way we make money. The catalyst for this transformative shift is Artificial Intelligence (AI). In this book, "AI Profits Unveiled: A Blueprint for Earning with Artificial Intelligence," we embark on a journey to explore the incredible opportunities that AI offers for those who are ready to seize them.

Artificial Intelligence, once the stuff of science fiction, is now a part of our daily lives. It powers our digital assistants, predicts our online shopping preferences, and drives autonomous vehicles. But AI's impact goes far beyond convenience and automation; it is a groundbreaking force that has the potential to generate substantial profits for individuals, businesses, and investors.

The purpose of this book is to demystify AI, offering you a comprehensive guide to understanding, harnessing, and profiting from its capabilities. We'll begin by unraveling the complexity of AI, breaking it down into understandable components. You don't need to be a computer scientist or data scientist to benefit from AI; we will explain the fundamental concepts in plain language.

We'll also dive into the practical aspects of building, deploying, and marketing AI solutions. This book is not just for tech enthusiasts; it's for entrepreneurs seeking new revenue streams, investors looking for promising opportunities, and professionals who want to stay ahead in a world that's rapidly becoming AI-driven.

CHAPTER 1
Demystifying Artificial Intelligence

Artificial Intelligence (AI) is a term that often conjures up images of futuristic robots and complex algorithms, shrouded in mystery and complexity. In this chapter, we aim to peel back the layers of mystique surrounding AI, making it accessible to everyone, regardless of their technical background.

1. What Is Artificial Intelligence?

At its core, AI refers to the ability of machines or computer systems to perform tasks that typically require human intelligence. These tasks include problem-solving, learning from experience, recognizing patterns, understanding natural language, and making decisions. AI can be broken down into two primary categories:

Narrow AI (Weak AI): This form of AI is designed for a specific task. It excels in performing that task but lacks the general intelligence and adaptability of humans.

General AI (Strong AI): General AI is the kind of artificial intelligence that has human-like cognitive abilities and can perform a wide range of tasks, essentially emulating human intelligence across various domains. It's a concept that remains more theoretical at this stage.

2. The AI Spectrum

AI exists on a spectrum, ranging from rule-based systems to machine learning and deep learning. Understanding this spectrum is essential for grasping how AI can be applied to different problems. Here's a breakdown:

Rule-Based Systems: These are AI systems that operate on predefined rules and logic. They are not adaptive and rely on specific instructions.

Machine Learning (ML): ML is a subset of AI that allows systems to learn from data. It can be categorized into supervised learning, unsupervised learning, and reinforcement learning.

Deep Learning: A subfield of ML, deep learning involves neural networks with multiple layers. It's responsible for many of the remarkable achievements in AI, such as image and speech recognition.

3. AI in Our Daily Lives

You might be surprised to learn just how much AI is already integrated into our daily lives:

Virtual Assistants: Siri, Alexa, and Google Assistant are AI-powered virtual assistants that can answer questions, perform tasks, and interact in natural language.

Recommendation Systems: AI algorithms power recommendations on platforms like Netflix and Amazon, suggesting content and products based on your previous choices.

Chatbots: Many businesses use AI chatbots to provide customer support and answer inquiries.

Healthcare: AI is employed in medical diagnostics, drug discovery, and treatment recommendations.

Finance: AI algorithms help with fraud detection, risk assessment, and algorithmic trading.

4. The Building Blocks of AI

To understand AI, you need to familiarize yourself with some of the key building blocks:

Data: Data is the lifeblood of AI. It includes structured and unstructured information that AI systems use for training, learning, and decision-making.

Algorithms: Algorithms are the step-by-step instructions that guide AI systems in performing tasks. The choice of the right algorithm is crucial in AI development.

Training Data: AI models require training data to learn patterns and make predictions. The quality and quantity of training data are critical.

5. What AI Is Not

It's also important to clarify what AI is not. AI is not sentient; it does not have consciousness, emotions, or self-awareness. AI operates based on the data and algorithms it's trained on, and it doesn't possess understanding or intention in the way humans do.

In the following chapters, we will delve deeper into the practical aspects of AI, from identifying opportunities and mastering data to building, deploying, and monetizing AI solutions. The goal is to empower you with the knowledge and tools needed to navigate the AI landscape and harness its profit-generating potential. AI is not reserved for a select few; it is a transformative force accessible to all who are willing to learn and innovate.

CHAPTER 2

Identifying Lucrative AI Ventures

One of the key steps in making money with artificial intelligence is to identify lucrative AI ventures. Whether you are an entrepreneur looking for a new business idea, an investor seeking opportunities, or a professional aiming to integrate AI into your existing work, understanding how to identify the right AI ventures is crucial. In this chapter, we will explore the process of recognizing profitable AI opportunities.

1. Market Research and Trends

Before diving into the world of AI, it's essential to conduct thorough market research and stay up-to-date with industry trends. Here's how to get started:

Market Analysis: Begin by analyzing the current market landscape. Identify industries and sectors where AI is already making an impact. Consider the potential for AI to disrupt traditional business models.

Market Growth: Look at market projections and growth rates. AI is a rapidly expanding field, and understanding where it's expected to grow the most can guide your decision-making.

Competitive Landscape: Examine existing players in the market. Who are the key competitors, and what are they doing with AI? Identifying gaps and opportunities is often easier when you understand the competitive dynamics.

Niche Markets: Sometimes, the most profitable AI ventures are found in niche markets or industries that are less explored. These areas can provide a competitive edge.

2. Identifying Industry-Specific Opportunities

AI can be applied across various industries, and the opportunities can vary significantly from one sector to another. Here are some examples of industry-specific AI opportunities:

Healthcare: AI can be used for medical diagnostics, drug discovery, patient care optimization, and telemedicine.

Finance: In the financial sector, AI can assist with fraud detection, algorithmic trading, credit risk assessment, and customer service.

Retail: AI powers recommendation systems, inventory management, and cashier-less stores.

Manufacturing: AI can enhance automation, predictive maintenance, quality control, and supply chain optimization.

Agriculture: Precision agriculture with AI helps in crop monitoring, yield prediction, and resource optimization.

Transportation: Autonomous vehicles and smart traffic management are examples of AI applications in transportation.

Education: AI-driven personalized learning platforms and intelligent tutoring systems are transforming education.

Energy: In the energy sector, AI contributes to grid optimization, predictive maintenance of equipment, and renewable energy management.

Entertainment: AI is used for content recommendation, video game development, and virtual reality experiences.

3. Identifying Specific AI Use Cases

To identify lucrative AI ventures, it's essential to understand the specific use cases and problems that AI can solve within the chosen industry. This involves:

Needs Assessment: Conduct a needs assessment to identify pain points and challenges within the industry or market you are targeting. Talk to potential customers or end-users to understand their problems.

AI Feasibility: Assess whether AI can provide practical solutions to these problems. This may require discussions with AI experts or data scientists.

Cost-Benefit Analysis: Evaluate the potential return on investment (ROI) of implementing AI solutions. Consider factors like reduced costs, increased revenue, and improved efficiency.

4. Staying Updated with AI Trends

AI is a rapidly evolving field, and staying updated with the latest trends and breakthroughs is crucial for identifying profitable ventures. Subscribe to AI-related publications, attend conferences, and participate in AI communities to keep your knowledge current.

5. Consider Ethical and Societal Implications

When identifying AI ventures, it's important to consider the ethical and societal implications of the technology. AI should be used for the betterment of society, and understanding the potential consequences of AI applications is essential.

In the following chapters, we will delve deeper into how to take your AI venture from the idea stage to a profitable business, including data collection and preparation, building AI models, deployment strategies, and monetization strategies. The key takeaway from this chapter is that identifying lucrative AI ventures involves a combination of market research, industry analysis, problem identification, and a keen understanding of AI's potential and limitations. With the right approach, you can position yourself to capitalize on the ever-expanding opportunities in the world of artificial intelligence.

CHAPTER 3
Data: The Lifeblood of AI Profit

Data is the lifeblood of artificial intelligence. It serves as the foundation upon which AI models are built, enabling them to learn, make predictions, and drive profits. In this chapter, we will explore the critical role that data plays in AI and how to harness its power to generate profits.

1. Understanding the Significance of Data

Training AI Models: AI models, whether they are for natural language processing, image recognition, or predictive analytics, require vast amounts of data to be trained effectively. This data is used to teach the model to recognize patterns and make accurate predictions.

Generalization: Data allows AI models to generalize from the information they've been exposed to. In other words, they can apply what they've learned to new, unseen data.

Iterative Improvement: AI models often improve with more data and exposure to real-world scenarios. The iterative nature of AI learning means that data remains a continuous source of improvement.

Decision-Making: In various applications, AI is used to make important decisions. The quality and relevance of the data directly impact the quality of those decisions.

2. Types of Data in AI

Data in the context of AI can be categorized into the following types:

Structured Data: This type of data is highly organized and easy to search, analyze, and process. Examples include data stored in spreadsheets and relational databases.

Unstructured Data: Unstructured data lacks a predefined structure and includes text, images, audio, and video. This type of data presents challenges in terms of analysis but is invaluable for many AI applications.

Semi-Structured Data: Semi-structured data falls somewhere in between. It has some structure, but it doesn't fit neatly into traditional databases. Examples include XML and JSON data.

3. Data Collection and Sourcing

To harness the power of data for AI profit, you must consider the following:

Data Sources: Identify the sources from which you will collect data. This can include sources such as websites, APIs, sensors, databases, and user-generated content.

Data Ownership and Rights: Be mindful of data ownership and rights. Ensure that you have the necessary permissions and rights to use the data for your AI applications, especially if the data is collected from external sources.

Data Quality: The quality of data is paramount. Clean, accurate, and relevant data is essential for training AI models effectively.

4. Data Preprocessing

Data preprocessing is the stage where raw data is cleaned, transformed, and prepared for AI model training. It involves tasks such as:

Data Cleaning: Removing or correcting errors, inconsistencies, and outliers in the data.

Data Transformation: Converting data into a suitable format for AI algorithms. This may involve scaling, normalization, or one-hot encoding.

Feature Engineering: Selecting and creating relevant features that help the AI model make accurate predictions.

5. Data Security and Privacy

With the growing emphasis on data security and privacy, it's crucial to consider these aspects when dealing with data for AI profit:

Data Encryption: Protect sensitive data with encryption to prevent unauthorized access.

Compliance: Ensure that your data handling practices comply with relevant data protection regulations, such as GDPR (General Data Protection Regulation) or HIPAA (Health Insurance Portability and Accountability Act).

Ethical Considerations: Be mindful of the ethical implications of data usage, including issues related to bias and fairness.

In the chapters that follow, we'll explore how to leverage data to build AI models, deploy them profitably, and explore various monetization strategies. Data is not just the lifeblood of AI; it's the catalyst for turning AI into a profitable venture. Understanding how to collect, process, and use data effectively is a critical step on the path to AI-driven profits.

CHAPTER 4
Mastering Machine Learning

Machine learning is the heart of artificial intelligence. It's the technology that allows AI systems to learn from data and make predictions or decisions. In this chapter, we will explore the fundamentals of mastering machine learning, a crucial skill for anyone seeking to make money with AI.

1. Understanding the Core Concepts of Machine Learning

Machine learning is based on several fundamental concepts:

Training Data: Machine learning models learn from training data, which consists of input features and corresponding output labels. The model's goal is to learn a mapping from inputs to outputs.

Algorithms: Machine learning models rely on algorithms to learn from data. These algorithms are responsible for making predictions and improving over time.

Supervised, Unsupervised, and Reinforcement Learning: Machine learning can be categorized into three primary types. In supervised learning, models are trained with labeled data. In unsupervised learning, models work with unlabeled data to discover patterns. In reinforcement learning, models learn by interacting with an environment and receiving rewards or penalties.

2. Machine Learning Models and Algorithms

The choice of machine learning algorithm depends on the nature of the problem you are trying to solve. Some common machine learning algorithms include:

Linear Regression: Used for predicting a continuous output variable based on input features.

Decision Trees and Random Forests: Used for both classification and regression tasks, decision trees create a tree-like structure to make decisions.

Support Vector Machines (SVM): Used for classification tasks by finding a hyperplane that best separates data points.

Neural Networks: A fundamental component of deep learning, neural networks consist of interconnected layers of artificial neurons.

3. Supervised Learning

In supervised learning, you work with labeled data, where the model learns to make predictions based on examples. Key concepts include:

Training and Testing Data: The dataset is typically divided into training and testing sets. The model is trained on the training data and evaluated on the testing data.

Loss Function: A loss function measures the error between the model's predictions and the actual labels. The model aims to minimize this error.

Evaluation Metrics: Common evaluation metrics for supervised learning include accuracy, precision, recall, and F1 score for classification tasks, and mean squared error for regression tasks.

4. Unsupervised Learning

Unsupervised learning is about finding patterns and structure in unlabeled data. Key concepts include:

Clustering: Clustering algorithms group similar data points together. K-Means and Hierarchical Clustering are common techniques.

Dimensionality Reduction: These methods reduce the number of input features while preserving important information. Principal Component Analysis (PCA) is a widely used technique.

5. Reinforcement Learning

Reinforcement learning involves an agent learning to make sequences of decisions to maximize a reward signal. Concepts include:

Markov Decision Process (MDP): An MDP models the decision-making process in a reinforcement learning task.

Exploration vs. Exploitation: In reinforcement learning, the agent must balance exploring new actions and exploiting known actions to maximize cumulative rewards.

6. Hyperparameter Tuning and Model Selection

Choosing the right hyperparameters for a machine learning model is a critical step. Techniques like cross-validation and grid search help find the best hyperparameter settings.

7. Practical Machine Learning

Mastering machine learning involves hands-on practice. Work on real-world datasets and projects to apply what you've learned. Platforms like TensorFlow, scikit-learn, and PyTorch can help you implement machine learning algorithms.

In the following chapters, we will delve deeper into building AI models, data preprocessing, deployment strategies, and monetization strategies. Mastering machine learning is a foundational skill for making money with AI. It allows you to develop AI models that can drive profits in various domains, from healthcare to finance to e-commerce.

CHAPTER 5
AI Frame Work

To master the art of making money with artificial intelligence, you need a toolkit of essential tools and technologies. In this chapter, we'll explore the key software, frameworks, and platforms that are crucial for AI development and deployment.

1. Popular AI Frameworks

AI frameworks are software libraries that provide the tools and building blocks necessary for developing AI models. Some of the most popular AI frameworks include:

TensorFlow: Developed by Google, TensorFlow is an open-source deep learning framework that allows for the creation of neural networks and other machine learning models. It's known for its flexibility and scalability.

PyTorch: Developed by Facebook's AI Research lab, PyTorch is another powerful deep learning framework. It's appreciated for its dynamic computation graph and is often used in research.

scikit-learn: This Python library is essential for classical machine learning tasks. It offers a wide range of tools for data preprocessing, model selection, and evaluation.

Keras: Keras is an open-source neural network library written in Python. It is known for its user-friendly, high-level interface and its compatibility with both TensorFlow and Theano.

2. Cloud Services for AI

Cloud services provide scalable computing power and storage, making them invaluable for AI development. Major cloud providers offer AI-specific services, including:

Amazon Web Services (AWS): AWS offers a range of AI services, including SageMaker for building, training, and deploying machine learning models, and Rekognition for image and video analysis.

Google Cloud AI: Google Cloud provides various AI services, such as AI Platform for model deployment and AutoML for creating custom machine learning models.

Microsoft Azure AI: Azure offers AI solutions like Azure Machine Learning and Cognitive Services for tasks like natural language processing, computer vision, and more.

IBM Watson: Watson is IBM's AI platform, providing tools for data analysis, machine learning, and natural language understanding.

3. Data Storage and Management

Efficient data storage and management are essential for AI projects. Some key technologies include:

Databases: Relational databases like PostgreSQL and MySQL, as well as NoSQL databases like MongoDB and Cassandra, are commonly used for storing structured and unstructured data.

Data Lakes: Data lakes, such as AWS S3 and Azure Data Lake Storage, are used for storing large volumes of diverse data types in their raw form.

Data Warehouses: Data warehouses like Amazon Redshift and Google BigQuery are designed for high-performance querying and analysis of structured data.

4. Development Environments

An integrated development environment (IDE) can streamline your AI development process:

Jupyter Notebook: Jupyter is a popular open-source web application that allows you to create and share documents that contain live code, equations, visualizations, and narrative text. It's widely used in data science and AI.

PyCharm: PyCharm is a Python-specific integrated development environment that provides features for code analysis, debugging, and testing.

Visual Studio Code: VS Code is a versatile code editor that supports various programming languages and offers extensive extensions for AI and data science.

5. Data Preprocessing Tools

Effective data preprocessing is essential for AI. Tools such as Pandas and NumPy in Python are widely used for data manipulation and cleaning.

6. Version Control

Version control systems like Git are crucial for tracking changes in your AI projects, collaborating with others, and maintaining code integrity.

7. Libraries and Packages

In addition to the frameworks mentioned earlier, there are many libraries and packages tailored to specific AI tasks. Some examples include NLTK and spaCy for natural language processing, OpenCV for computer vision, and Gensim for text analysis.

8. Visualization Tools

Visualization tools like Matplotlib and Seaborn make it easier to explore and communicate insights from your data.

9. Containerization and Orchestration

Containerization tools like Docker and container orchestration platforms like Kubernetes are important for deploying AI applications in a consistent and scalable manner.

These essential tools and technologies form the backbone of your AI toolkit. As you progress in your AI journey, you may explore additional specialized tools and platforms that align with your specific goals and projects. In the chapters that follow, we will delve into the practical aspects of building and deploying AI models, as well as strategies for monetizing your AI ventures. Your proficiency with these tools and technologies will be instrumental in translating your AI expertise into financial gains.

CHAPTER 6

Building High-Impact AI Models

Building high-impact AI models is a fundamental step on the path to making money with artificial intelligence. In this chapter, we'll explore the key components and strategies for creating AI models that deliver real value and profitability.

1. Data Labeling and Cleaning

Data Labeling: For supervised learning tasks, data labeling is essential. You need labeled data to train your AI model. This process involves assigning meaningful labels or categories to the data.

Data Cleaning: Data is rarely perfect. Data cleaning involves removing or correcting errors, dealing with missing values, and addressing inconsistencies in the dataset.

2. Feature Engineering

Feature engineering is the process of selecting, creating, and transforming features (variables) in your dataset to improve the performance of your AI model. It's a critical step in model development. Considerations include:

Feature Selection: Choosing the most relevant features for your model and removing irrelevant ones.

Feature Creation: Sometimes, you may need to create new features that capture important information from the data.

Feature Transformation: Transforming features through techniques like scaling, normalization, or one-hot encoding.

3. Model Selection and Hyperparameter Tuning

Choosing the right machine learning or deep learning model for your task is crucial. Some models may be more suitable for classification tasks, while others are better for regression. Key steps include:

Model Selection: Experiment with different models and select the one that performs best for your specific task.

Hyperparameter Tuning: Adjust the hyperparameters of your model to optimize its performance. This may involve grid search or Bayesian optimization.

4. Model Training and Evaluation

Training: Train your model on the labeled data using an appropriate algorithm. This process involves optimizing the model's internal parameters to make accurate predictions.

Evaluation: Assess your model's performance using evaluation metrics that are relevant to your specific task. For classification, metrics like accuracy, precision, recall, and F1 score are common. For regression, mean squared error and mean absolute error are often used.

5. Cross-Validation

Cross-validation is a technique used to assess how well your model will generalize to unseen data. It involves splitting your dataset into multiple subsets and training and evaluating your model on different combinations of these subsets.

6. Ensuring Model Robustness

Model robustness is essential to ensure your AI model performs well in various scenarios:

Overfitting and Underfitting: Avoid overfitting, where the model performs well on the training data but poorly on new data. Likewise, avoid underfitting, where the model is too simplistic to capture the underlying patterns.

Regularization: Techniques like L1 and L2 regularization can help prevent overfitting.

Ensemble Methods: Consider using ensemble methods like bagging and boosting to improve model performance and robustness.

7. Interpretability and Explainability

In some applications, model interpretability and explainability are important. Understanding why a model makes a certain prediction can be critical in fields like healthcare, finance, and law.

8. Validation and Testing

Before deploying your AI model, you need to validate it on a separate dataset to ensure it performs well in a real-world environment.

9. Continuous Improvement and Monitoring

AI models are not static; they require continuous improvement and monitoring to maintain their performance. Strategies for model retraining and ongoing maintenance are essential.Building high-impact AI models involves a combination of data preparation, feature engineering, model selection, and evaluation. The process is iterative, and your models will likely improve with experience. In the subsequent chapters, we will delve into strategies for deploying AI models and monetizing your AI ventures, turning your expertise into financial gains.

CHAPTER 7

Bringing AI to Market

Once you've developed a high-impact AI model, the next step is to bring it to market. Successfully deploying your AI solution is crucial to start generating revenue. In this chapter, we'll explore strategies for bringing AI to market effectively.

1. Deployment Strategies

On-Premises Deployment: In some cases, you may choose to deploy your AI solution directly on the client's hardware or servers. This approach provides more control over data and infrastructure but may require more extensive setup and maintenance.

Cloud Deployment: Cloud-based deployment, using services like AWS, Azure, or Google Cloud, offers scalability, flexibility, and ease of management. It's a popular choice for many AI applications.

Edge Deployment: Deploying AI models on edge devices, such as IoT devices or mobile phones, is advantageous when real-time processing is essential or when data privacy is a concern.

2. Scalability and Cost Considerations

Consider the scalability and cost aspects of your deployment strategy:

Scalability: Ensure your AI solution can handle increasing workloads as your user base grows. Cloud services provide scalability but may involve additional costs.

Cost Management: Monitor and manage your operating costs carefully, especially if you're using cloud services. Implement cost-saving measures like auto-scaling and resource optimization.

3. Continuous Monitoring and Updates

Your AI solution is not a one-time deployment; it requires continuous monitoring and updates:

Monitoring: Implement monitoring systems to track the performance of your AI solution. Monitor for anomalies, errors, and security breaches.

Maintenance: Regularly update your model with new data to keep it relevant and accurate. Address issues and bugs promptly to maintain quality.

4. Data Privacy and Security

Data privacy and security are paramount when bringing AI to market:

Data Encryption: Implement data encryption techniques to protect sensitive information in transit and at rest.

Access Control: Restrict access to your AI system to authorized personnel and ensure data is only accessible by those with proper permissions.

Regulatory Compliance: Comply with data protection regulations, such as GDPR, HIPAA, or industry-specific standards.

5. User Experience and Interface

A user-friendly interface can significantly impact the success of your AI solution:

User-Centered Design: Design your interface with the end-users in mind. It should be intuitive and efficient.

Feedback Mechanisms: Include feedback mechanisms to collect user input and continuously improve your solution.

6. Documentation and Support

Comprehensive documentation and user support are vital:

Documentation: Provide clear documentation to help users understand how to use your AI solution effectively.

Customer Support: Offer customer support, including assistance with setup, troubleshooting, and questions.

7. Marketing and Promotion

Effective marketing is crucial to attract users and customers:

Digital Marketing: Use online marketing channels, such as social media, content marketing, and search engine optimization, to promote your AI solution.

Networking: Attend conferences, webinars, and industry events to network with potential customers and partners.

Case Studies: Share success stories and case studies showcasing the value of your AI solution.

8. Building Partnerships

Consider forming partnerships with organizations that can help you reach a wider audience or provide complementary services. Partnerships can accelerate market entry and growth.

9. Pricing and Monetization Strategies

Determine how you will monetize your AI solution:

Subscription Models: Charge users a recurring fee to access your AI solution.

Licensing: License your AI software to other businesses for a fee.

Pay-per-Use: Charge users based on the volume or frequency of their use of your solution.

Freemium Model: Offer a basic version of your AI solution for free and charge for premium features or additional services.

10. Legal Considerations

Address legal aspects, including:

Intellectual Property: Protect your AI model and related software with patents or copyrights.

Contracts: Use clear contracts and terms of service with users and clients to define responsibilities, usage rights, and liabilities.

Bringing AI to market requires a well-thought-out strategy that encompasses deployment, scalability, cost management, security, user experience, marketing, partnerships, pricing, and legal considerations. By following these strategies, you can effectively introduce your AI solution to the market and work toward realizing its profit potential.

CHAPTER 8

Monetization Strategies

Monetizing your artificial intelligence (AI) solutions is the key to turning your AI expertise into financial gains. In this chapter, we'll explore various monetization strategies to help you generate revenue from your AI ventures.

1. Licensing and SaaS Models

Licensing: License your AI software to other businesses or individuals. You can offer different licensing models, such as one-time licenses, annual subscriptions, or usage-based licenses.

Software as a Service (SaaS): Deliver your AI solution as a cloud-based SaaS platform. Users pay a recurring fee to access and use the service, often on a subscription basis.

2. Data Monetization

Data Sales: If your AI solution generates valuable data, you can monetize that data by selling it to other businesses or researchers.

Data Sharing: Collaborate with other organizations to share data in a mutually beneficial way. Data-sharing agreements can generate revenue and improve your AI models.

3. Consultation and Customization Services

Offer consultation services related to your AI solution. Businesses may require assistance in implementing and customizing AI models for their specific needs. Charge for your expertise and services.

4. White Labeling and Reselling

Allow other businesses to resell your AI solution under their own brand. This can expand your reach and generate revenue through licensing agreements with these resellers.

5. Subscription Models

Implement subscription models that offer premium features or additional services to users who subscribe. Freemium models, where a basic version is free, can encourage users to upgrade to a paid subscription.

6. In-App Purchases

If your AI solution is integrated into mobile apps or software, consider offering in-app purchases for advanced AI features or functionalities.

7. Advertising and Affiliate Marketing

If your AI solution attracts a large user base, you can monetize through advertising, sponsored content, or affiliate marketing. Display ads or promote products and services relevant to your users.

8. Partnerships and Joint Ventures

Collaborate with other businesses or organizations to create joint ventures or partnerships. You can co-develop AI solutions and share the revenue generated from these ventures.

9. Intellectual Property Licensing

If your AI models or algorithms have unique and valuable characteristics, consider licensing them to other organizations or industries for a fee.

10. Crowdsourcing and Crowdfunding

Use crowdsourcing platforms to fund your AI projects. Platforms like Kickstarter or Indiegogo can help you secure funding from interested individuals.

11. Grants and Research Funding

Seek research grants and funding from government agencies, research institutions, and foundations. These grants can support the development of AI projects and generate income.

12. Affiliate Programs

If your AI solution integrates with e-commerce or online platforms, consider participating in affiliate programs to earn commissions on sales generated through your AI solution.

13. Premium Content and Services

Offer premium content or services within your AI solution. Users can pay for access to advanced features, personalized recommendations, or exclusive content.

14. Pay-Per-Use Models

Charge users based on their actual usage of your AI solution. This can be particularly effective for data analysis and processing services.

15. Industry-Specific Monetization

In certain industries, there are unique monetization opportunities. For example, in healthcare, you can charge for diagnostic AI services. In finance, you can monetize algorithmic trading models.

16. Non-Profit and Research Grants

If your AI solution has social or research value, you may secure non-profit grants and research funding to support your work.

Selecting the right monetization strategy depends on the nature of your AI solution, your target audience, and your business goals. It's common for AI ventures to use a combination of these strategies to maximize revenue streams. As you explore monetization opportunities, keep your users' needs and expectations in mind to strike the right balance between profitability and user satisfaction.

CHAPTER 9

Marketing Your AI Enterprise

Once you've developed and deployed your AI solutions, marketing becomes crucial to reach your target audience and generate revenue. In this chapter, we'll explore strategies for effectively marketing your AI enterprise.

1. Define Your Target Audience

Identify and define your target audience. Understand their needs, pain points, and preferences. Tailor your marketing strategies to address their specific concerns.

2. Establish an Online Presence

Create a professional website and maintain a strong online presence. Your website should provide information about your AI solutions, case studies, testimonials, and contact details.

3. Content Marketing

Produce high-quality content that showcases your expertise in AI. This content can include blog posts, whitepapers, case studies, and educational materials. Content marketing helps establish your authority in the field.

4. Search Engine Optimization (SEO)

Optimize your website and content for search engines. Implement relevant keywords, meta tags, and backlinks to improve your search engine rankings and increase organic traffic.

5. Social Media Marketing

Use social media platforms to connect with your audience. Share content, engage in discussions, and build a community around your AI solutions. Platforms like LinkedIn, Twitter, and Facebook are valuable for B2B marketing.

6. Email Marketing

Build an email list of potential customers and keep them informed about your AI solutions, updates, and promotions. Use email marketing to nurture leads and convert them into customers.

7. Paid Advertising

Invest in paid advertising campaigns, such as Google Ads or social media advertising. Pay-per-click (PPC) campaigns can help you target specific keywords and demographics.

8. Online Webinars and Workshops

Host webinars and online workshops to demonstrate the value of your AI solutions. Educate your audience about the benefits of AI and how your offerings can solve their problems.

9. Networking and Conferences

Attend industry conferences, seminars, and networking events. These provide opportunities to meet potential customers, partners, and investors. Share your AI expertise through presentations or panel discussions.

10. Case Studies and Testimonials

Publish case studies and gather testimonials from satisfied customers. Real-world examples of successful AI implementations can build trust and credibility.

11. Influencer Marketing

Collaborate with influencers or thought leaders in the AI and technology space. They can help promote your AI solutions to their followers and provide third-party validation.

12. Online Communities and Forums

Participate in online communities and forums relevant to your industry. Answer questions, provide value, and establish your presence as an AI expert.

13. PR and Media Outreach

Reach out to industry-specific media outlets, tech blogs, and news websites. Share your AI success stories, new product launches, and company achievements.

14. Referral Programs

Implement referral programs to encourage existing customers to refer new clients. Offer incentives or discounts to those who refer successful leads.

15. Analytics and Tracking

Use analytics tools to track the performance of your marketing efforts. Measure key performance indicators (KPIs) to assess the effectiveness of your strategies and make data-driven improvements.

16. Partnerships and Alliances

Form strategic partnerships with other companies in related industries. These partnerships can open up new marketing channels and expand your customer base.

17. Customer Education

Educate your customers about the value of AI and how to use your solutions effectively. Host workshops, webinars, and create educational content.

Effective marketing is an ongoing process. Continuously adapt and refine your strategies based on data and feedback. As you execute your marketing plan, focus on providing value, building trust, and demonstrating how your AI solutions can address real-world challenges. Your marketing efforts will play a pivotal role in the success and profitability of your AI enterprise.

CHAPTER 10

Real-World Success Stories

In this chapter, we'll explore real-world success stories that highlight how artificial intelligence (AI) has been leveraged to solve complex problems, create value, and drive profitability in various industries. These stories serve as inspiration and examples of the immense potential AI holds for businesses and individuals.

1. Healthcare: IBM Watson for Oncology

Problem: The field of oncology involves an overwhelming amount of medical data and research, making it challenging for oncologists to stay updated on the latest treatments and recommendations.

Solution: IBM Watson for Oncology is an AI platform that uses natural language processing and machine learning to analyze vast amounts of medical literature and clinical trial data. It provides personalized treatment recommendations to oncologists based on a patient's medical records and the latest research.

Result: By assisting oncologists in treatment decisions, IBM Watson for Oncology has improved the accuracy and efficiency of cancer care. It has been deployed in multiple countries and healthcare institutions, positively impacting patient outcomes.

2. Finance: Algorithmic Trading

Problem: Financial markets are highly complex and dynamic, making it challenging for human traders to make real-time decisions and execute trades efficiently.

Solution: Algorithmic trading involves the use of AI and machine learning models to analyze market data and execute trades at high speeds. These algorithms can identify profitable opportunities and execute orders with minimal human intervention.

Result: Algorithmic trading has become a standard practice in the financial industry. It allows firms to make trades at lightning speed, respond to market changes in real time, and optimize their trading strategies. Many financial institutions have reported substantial profits through algorithmic trading.

3. Retail: Amazon's Recommendation System

Problem: Online retailers face the challenge of helping customers discover relevant products in vast catalogs, leading to low conversion rates and unsatisfied customers.

Solution: Amazon's recommendation system uses machine learning to analyze customer behavior, past purchases, and browsing history to suggest personalized product recommendations. These recommendations appear on the website, in emails, and on the Amazon app.

Result: Amazon's recommendation system has significantly contributed to the company's success. It drives a substantial portion of Amazon's sales by helping customers discover products they might not have found otherwise. This demonstrates the power of AI in increasing revenue and customer satisfaction.

4. Autonomous Vehicles: Waymo (formerly Google Self-Driving Car Project)

Problem: Road accidents and human error are significant challenges in the transportation industry. Autonomous vehicles aim to address these issues by leveraging AI for safe and efficient driving.

Solution: Waymo, a subsidiary of Alphabet, developed a self-driving car platform that combines sensors, computer vision, machine learning, and extensive real-world testing. The AI system allows vehicles to perceive their environment and make driving decisions without human intervention.

Result: Waymo has made substantial progress in autonomous driving technology. They've deployed autonomous taxis and are testing autonomous trucks, contributing to the future of safe and efficient transportation.

5. Manufacturing: Predictive Maintenance with General Electric

Problem: Manufacturing plants often face unexpected machine breakdowns and downtime, resulting in production losses and maintenance costs.

Solution: General Electric (GE) has implemented AI-driven predictive maintenance solutions that analyze sensor data from industrial equipment. Machine learning models predict when equipment is likely to fail, enabling proactive maintenance.

Result: GE's predictive maintenance has reduced unplanned downtime and increased the reliability of industrial machinery. By preventing costly breakdowns and optimizing maintenance schedules, businesses can save substantial amounts and improve their profitability.

6. Agriculture: Precision Farming with John Deere

Problem: Agriculture faces the challenge of optimizing resource use while increasing crop yields and quality.

Solution: John Deere, a leading agriculture machinery manufacturer, uses AI-driven precision farming technology. This technology integrates data from sensors, satellites, and drones to provide insights into soil conditions, weather patterns, and crop health.

Farmers can make data-informed decisions about planting, harvesting, and resource allocation.

Result: Precision farming has improved crop yields, reduced resource waste, and increased the profitability of farms. It showcases how AI can enhance traditional industries through data-driven decision-making.

These real-world success stories illustrate the transformative power of AI across various sectors, from healthcare to finance to agriculture. They demonstrate that AI can not only solve complex problems but also drive profitability and create substantial value for businesses and society as a whole. As AI continues to advance, its potential for real-world impact and success stories is only expected to grow.

CHAPTER 10

Legal and Ethical Considerations in AI

As you delve into the world of artificial intelligence (AI) and aim to make money with AI applications, it's essential to be aware of the legal and ethical considerations that come with this territory. AI presents unique challenges and responsibilities that need to be addressed. In this chapter, we'll explore the key legal and ethical considerations.

1. Data Privacy

Data privacy is a paramount concern when dealing with AI, particularly if your application involves handling personal or sensitive data. Legal frameworks like the European Union's General Data Protection Regulation (GDPR) and the U.S. Health Insurance Portability and Accountability Act (HIPAA) impose strict requirements on data handling, storage, and protection.

2. Bias and Fairness

AI systems can inadvertently perpetuate biases present in the data they are trained on. It's essential to ensure that AI models are fair and unbiased, particularly in domains like finance, hiring, and criminal justice. Addressing bias and fairness is both an ethical and legal obligation.

3. Intellectual Property

If you've developed novel AI algorithms, models, or software, it's crucial to protect your intellectual property with patents, copyrights, or trademarks. You may also need to respect the intellectual property rights of others when using AI tools and data.

4. Liability and Accountability

Determining liability for AI systems can be complex. Who is responsible if an autonomous vehicle causes an accident, or if a medical AI makes a diagnostic error? Understanding the legal framework for liability and establishing clear accountability is essential.

5. Regulation and Compliance

AI is subject to a growing number of regulations. Staying compliant with regional and industry-specific rules is critical to avoid legal complications. This includes adhering to regulations in healthcare, finance, and autonomous vehicles, among others.

6. Transparency and Explainability

Transparency in AI decision-making is essential for both ethical and legal reasons. Users and stakeholders need to understand how AI systems arrive at their conclusions. This is especially crucial in contexts like healthcare and finance.

7. Informed Consent

In situations where AI processes personal data, obtaining informed consent from users is essential. This means individuals should be aware of what data is being collected, how it will be used, and have the choice to opt in or out.

8. Security and Cybersecurity

AI applications often involve processing sensitive data. Ensuring robust cybersecurity measures is both a legal requirement and an ethical responsibility to protect data from breaches and unauthorized access.

9. Ethical AI Development

Adhere to ethical guidelines and principles when developing AI systems. This includes considering the potential societal impact, ensuring transparency, minimizing harm, and addressing biases and fairness.

10. Ethical Decision-Making in AI

As a developer or business owner, consider the ethical implications of your AI applications. Be prepared to make difficult ethical decisions, such as when to prioritize human judgment over AI recommendations.

11. Ethical Considerations in AI Research

Researchers should follow ethical guidelines when conducting AI research, particularly in fields like machine learning and natural language processing, to prevent misuse and unintended harm.

12. Compliance with International Standards

Adhere to international standards and best practices, such as ISO/IEC standards for AI, to ensure the quality, safety, and ethical usage of AI technology.

Navigating the legal and ethical landscape of AI can be complex, but it's essential for building trust with users, partners, and regulatory authorities. Be proactive in addressing these considerations, and consider seeking legal counsel or ethics experts when needed. By prioritizing legal and ethical principles, you can create AI applications that not only generate revenue but also contribute positively to society and the industry.

CHAPTER 11

Scaling Your AI Business

Scaling your artificial intelligence (AI) business is a pivotal step in maximizing profitability and long-term success. In this chapter, we will explore strategies and considerations for growing your AI venture.

1. Develop a Scalable Business Model

Ensure that your business model is designed for scalability. This includes a clear plan for how your AI solutions can serve an increasing number of customers without proportionally increasing costs.

2. Investment and Funding

Scaling often requires financial investment. Seek funding through various sources such as venture capital, angel investors, loans, or grants. These funds can be used to hire talent, expand infrastructure, and support marketing efforts.

3. Talent Acquisition

Hiring the right talent is crucial for growth. As your business scales, you may need data scientists, software engineers, sales and marketing professionals, and customer support staff. Build a team that can support your expanding operations.

4. Partnerships and Alliances

Form strategic partnerships with other businesses in your industry or related fields. These partnerships can help you access new customer segments and distribution channels, accelerating your growth.

5. Expanding Market Reach

Consider expanding your market reach by targeting new geographical areas or industries. Localizing your AI solutions for different markets can open up additional revenue streams.

6. Product Diversification

Diversify your AI product offerings to cater to a wider audience. This can include developing new features, specialized solutions, or entering adjacent markets.

7. Customer Retention

While acquiring new customers is essential, retaining existing ones is equally important. A focus on customer satisfaction, support, and ongoing value can reduce churn and lead to increased revenue from loyal clients.

8. Automate Routine Processes

Leverage AI to automate routine business processes. This not only reduces operational costs but also allows your team to focus on strategic growth initiatives.

9. Data Monetization

If your AI solutions generate valuable data, explore opportunities to monetize that data by selling it or sharing it with research organizations, marketers, or industry partners.

10. Continuous Innovation

Stay at the forefront of AI technology by continuously innovating. This includes R&D efforts to improve existing solutions and create new ones that address emerging market needs.

11. Cloud Services and Scalability

Utilize cloud-based services to scale your infrastructure and operations as needed. Cloud platforms offer flexibility and scalability without the need for substantial upfront investments in hardware and data centers.

12. Customer Feedback and Adaptation

Actively gather and act upon customer feedback. Adapting your AI solutions based on user input is essential for meeting changing needs and maintaining customer satisfaction.

13. Data Security and Compliance

Ensure that your data security and privacy measures are scalable. As your customer base grows, data protection and regulatory compliance become even more critical.

14. Marketing and Brand Building

Invest in marketing efforts that align with your growth strategy. Focus on expanding your brand's visibility, reaching new audiences, and showcasing your AI solutions' value.

15. Effective Sales Strategies

Implement effective sales strategies that cater to the needs of your target audience. This may involve hiring dedicated sales teams or refining your sales processes.

16. Legal and Regulatory Considerations

As your business scales, you may encounter more complex legal and regulatory challenges. Ensure that your legal and compliance efforts can scale with your business.

Scaling an AI business requires careful planning, resource allocation, and a clear growth strategy. Be prepared for both the challenges and opportunities that come with expansion. By continually adapting and optimizing your approach, you can position your AI business for sustainable growth and profitability.

CHAPTER 12

The Path to Profitability

Achieving profitability with your artificial intelligence (AI) endeavors is a journey that involves careful planning, execution, and adaptation. In this chapter, we will outline the key steps to guide you along the path to profitability with AI.

1. Define Clear Objectives

Start by setting clear and specific objectives for your AI projects. Understand what you want to achieve, whether it's revenue generation, cost reduction, or improved efficiency.

2. Validate Market Demand

Before investing significant resources, validate the market demand for your AI solution. Identify potential customers and gather feedback to ensure there is a genuine need for your product.

3. Cost Control

Control costs from the outset. Efficient budgeting and cost management are critical to profitability. Be mindful of expenses related to data acquisition, infrastructure, talent, and marketing.

4. Pricing Strategy

Determine a pricing strategy that reflects the value your AI solution provides. This can involve various models such as subscription pricing, one-time licensing, or pay-per-use.

5. Monetization Channels

Identify the most suitable monetization channels for your AI solutions. Explore options like licensing, subscriptions, data sales, partnerships, and consulting services.

6. Lean Development

Embrace lean development methodologies to minimize waste and maximize efficiency in the development process. Continuously test and iterate to improve your AI solutions.

7. Data Management

Efficient data management is crucial for AI projects. Ensure that you collect, store, and process data in a cost-effective and secure manner.

8. Marketing and Promotion

Invest in marketing efforts that align with your budget and objectives. Focus on channels and strategies that are most likely to reach your target audience effectively.

9. Customer Acquisition and Retention

Acquiring new customers is essential, but retaining existing ones can be more cost-effective. Implement customer retention strategies and prioritize customer satisfaction.

10. Strategic Alliances

Form strategic alliances and partnerships with businesses that complement your AI solutions. These alliances can expand your reach and generate additional revenue streams.

11. Scalability and Efficiency

Design your AI solutions with scalability and efficiency in mind. This enables you to accommodate growth without a linear increase in costs.

12. Innovation and R&D

Continuous innovation is key to maintaining a competitive edge. Allocate resources to research and development to improve your AI offerings and stay ahead of the competition.

13. Legal and Compliance

Stay compliant with legal and regulatory requirements. Address legal considerations early to avoid potential setbacks that could affect profitability.

14. Customer Support and Feedback

Provide excellent customer support and gather feedback from users. Understanding their needs and addressing issues promptly can lead to higher customer satisfaction and loyalty.

15. Track Key Performance Indicators (KPIs)

Monitor key performance indicators, such as customer acquisition cost, customer lifetime value, and churn rate. These metrics help you assess the health and profitability of your AI business.

16. Iterate and Optimize

Continuously iterate and optimize your AI solutions, business model, and processes based on data-driven insights. This iterative approach can lead to improved profitability over time.

17. Diversification

Consider diversifying your AI offerings to reach different market segments or industries. Multiple revenue streams can enhance profitability and reduce risk.

18. Focus on Core Competencies

Concentrate on your core competencies and avoid spreading resources too thin. Focus on what you do best and where you can generate the most value.

19. Exit Strategy

Have a clear exit strategy in mind, whether it involves selling the business, going public, or other options. A well-planned exit strategy can maximize the value of your AI venture.

The path to profitability with AI involves a combination of careful planning, effective execution, and continuous adaptation. By setting clear objectives, controlling costs, understanding your market, and maintaining a focus on customer satisfaction, you can work towards sustainable profitability and success in the AI industry.

gate the AI landscape. Packed with real-world case studies and insights into legal and ethical considerations, it equips entrepreneurs, investors, and professionals with the knowledge and strategies needed to thrive in the AI-powered world, ultimately unveiling the path to AI-driven profitability.

ABOUT THE AUTHOR

ALEX USIFO

Alex USIFO is An African entrepreneur and business magnate. He is best known for his involvement in several high-profile tech companies. Alex Usifo has an educational background in physics and economics.

Alex Usifo is known for his visionary approach to technology and innovation. My motivation is to drive advancements in technology that he believes will benefit humanity. I've been able to cover work covers a wide range of topics in the tech field, including electric vehicles, space exploration, renewable energy, artificial intelligence, and transportation infrastructure.

As an author, I have shared his thoughts and insights in various interviews, articles, and public speeches, providing a unique perspective on the future of technology and its impact on society. He has also been vocal about his concerns related to artificial intelligence and has contributed to discussions about its potential benefits and risks.